Animal Homes

by Janelle Cherrington

capstone
classroom

Let's visit a cliff. Who lives on it?

nest

An eagle lives on a cliff. It has eggs in its nest.

den

Let's visit a den. Who lives in it?

pup

A red fox lives in a den. It has one pup.

Who lives in a box hive? Bees live in it.

A bee can fly fast. It can zig and zag and zap!

He does his job well. A bee cannot zap him.